D0819040

The Unwritten Laws of Business

W. J. King

For information regarding special discounts for bulk purchases,

please contact BN Publishing

sales@bnpublishing.net

Contents

1

What the Beginner Needs to Learn at Once

Some years ago the author became very much impressed with the fact, which can be observed in any engineering organization, that the chief obstacles to the success of individual engineers or of the group comprising a unit were of a personal and administrative rather than a technical nature. It was apparent that both the author and his associates were getting into much more trouble by violating the unwritten laws of professional conduct than by committing technical sins against the well-documented laws of science. Since the former appeared to be indeed unwritten at that time, as regards any adequate and convenient text, the following "laws" were originally formulated and collected into a sort of scrapbook, to provide a set of "house rules," or a professional code, for a design-engineering section of a large manufacturing organization. Although they are admittedly fragmentary and incomplete, they are offered here for whatever they may be worth to younger men just starting their careers, and to older men who know these things perfectly well but who all too often fail to apply them in practice.

Just a few points should be emphasized: None of these "laws" is theoretical or imaginary, and however obvious and trite they may appear, their repeated violation is responsible for much of the frustration and embarrassment to which engineers everywhere are liable. In fact this paper is primarily a record, derived from direct observation over a period of seventeen years, of the experience of four engineering departments, three of them newly organized and struggling to establish themselves by the trial-and-error method. It has, however, been supplemented and confirmed by the experience of others as gathered from numerous discussions, lectures, and the literature, so that it most emphatically does not reflect the unique experience or characteristics of any one organization.

Furthermore, many of these rules are generalizations to which exceptions will occur in special circumstances. There is no thought of urging a slavish adherence to rules and red tape, for there is no substitute for judgment, and at times vigorous individual initiative is needed to cut through formalities in an emergency. But in many respects these laws are like the basic laws of society; they cannot be violated too often with impunity, notwithstanding striking exceptions in individual cases.

IN RELATION TO HIS WORK

However menial and trivial your early assignments may appear give them your best efforts. Many young engineers feel that the minor chores of a technical project are beneath their dignity and unworthy of their college training. They expect to prove their true worth in some major enterprise. Actually, the spirit and effectiveness with which you tackle your first humble tasks will very likely be carefully watched and may affect your entire career.

Occasionally a man will worry unduly about where his job is going to get him—whether it is sufficiently strategic or significant. Of course these are pertinent considerations and you would do well to take some stock of them, but by and large it is fundamentally true that if you take care of your present job well, the future will take care of itself. This is particularly so in the case of a large corporation, where executives are constantly searching for competent men to move up into more responsible positions. Success depends so largely upon personality, native ability, and vigorous, intelligent prosecution of any job that it is no exaggeration to say that your ultimate chances are much better if you do a good job on some minor detail than if you do a mediocre job as section head. Furthermore, it is also true that if you do not first make a good showing on your present job you are not likely to be given the opportunity of trying something else more to your liking.

There is always a premium upon the ability to get things done. This is a quality which may be achieved by various means under different circumstances. Specific aspects will be elaborated in some of the succeeding items. It can probably be reduced, however, to a combination of three basic characteristics, as follows:

(*a*) Energy, which is expressed in initiative to start things and aggressiveness to keep them moving briskly.

(*b*) Resourcefulness or ingenuity, i.e., the faculty for finding ways to accomplish the desired result, and

(*c*) Persistence (tenacity), which is the disposition to persevere in spite of difficulties, discouragement, or indifference.

This last quality is sometimes lacking in the make-up of brilliant engineers, to such an extent that their effectiveness is greatly reduced. Such dilettantes are known as "good starters but poor finishers." Or else it will be said of a man: "You can't take him too seriously; he'll be all steamed up over an idea today but tomorrow he will have dropped it and started chasing some other rainbow." Bear in mind, therefore, that it may be worth while finishing a job, if it has any merit, just for the sake of finishing it.

In carrying out a project do not wait for foremen, vendors, and others to deliver the goods; go after them and keep everlastingly after them. This is one of the first things a new man has to learn in entering a manufacturing organization. Many novices assume that it is sufficient to place the order and sit back and wait until the goods are delivered. The fact is that most jobs move in direct proportion to the amount of follow-up and *expediting* that is applied to them. Expediting means planning, investigating, promoting, and facilitating every step in the process. Cultivate the habit of looking immediately for some way around each obstacle encountered, some other recourse or expedient to keep the job rolling without losing momentum. There are ten-to-one differences between individuals in respect to what it takes to stop their drive when they set out to get something done.

On the other hand, the matter is occasionally overdone by overzealous individuals who make themselves obnoxious and antagonize everyone by their offensive browbeating tactics. Be careful about demanding action from another department. Too much insistence and agitation may result in more damage to a man's personal interests than could ever result from the miscarriage of the technical point involved.

Confirm your instructions and the other fellow's commitments in writing. Do not assume that the job will be done or the bargain kept just because the other fellow agreed to do it. Many people have poor memories, others are too busy, and almost everyone will take the matter a great deal more seriously if he sees it in writing. Of course there are exceptions, but at times it pays to mark a third party for a copy of the memo, as a witness.

When sent out on any complaint or other assignment stick with it and see it through to a successful finish. All too often a young engineer from the home office will leave a job half done or poorly done in order to catch a train or keep some other engagement. Wire the boss that you've got to stay over to clean up the job. Neither he nor the customer will like if it another man has to be sent out later to finish it up.

Avoid the very appearance of vacillation. One of the gravest in-

4

dictments of an engineer is to say: "His opinion at any time depends merely upon the last man with whom he has talked." Refrain from stating an opinion or promoting an undertaking until you have had a reasonable opportunity to obtain and study the facts. Thereafter see it through if at all possible, unless fresh evidence makes it folly to persist. Obviously the extremes of bullheadedness and dogmatism should be avoided, but remember that reversed decisions will be held against you.

Don't be timid—speak up—express yourself and promote your ideas. Every young man should read Emerson's essay on "Self Reliance." Too many new men seem to think that their job is simply to do what they're told to do, along the lines laid down by the boss. Of course there are times when it is very wise and prudent to keep your mouth shut, but, as a rule, it pays to express your point of view whenever you can contribute something. The quiet mousey individual who says nothing is usually credited with having nothing to say.

It frequently happens in any sort of undertaking that nobody is sure of just how the matter ought to be handled; it's a question of selecting some kind of program with a reasonable chance of success. This is commonly to be observed in engineering-office conferences. The first man to speak up with a definite and plausible proposal has better than an even chance of carrying the floor, provided only that the scheme is definite and plausible. (The "best" scheme usually cannot be recognized as such in advance.) It also happens that the man who talks most knowingly and confidently about the matter will very often end up with the assignment to carry out the project. If you do not want the job, keep your mouth shut and you'll be overlooked, but you'll also be overlooked when it comes time to assign larger responsibilities.

Before asking for approval of any major action, have a definite plan and program worked out to support it. Executives very generally and very properly will refuse to approve any proposed under-

5

taking that is not well planned and thought through as regards the practical details of its execution. Quite often a young man will propose a project without having worked out the means of accomplishing it, or weighing the actual advantages against the difficulties and costs. This is the difference between a "well-considered" and a "half-baked" scheme.

Strive for conciseness and clarity in oral or written reports. If there is one bane of an executive's existence, it is the man who takes a half hour of rambling discourse to tell him what could be said in one sentence of twenty words. There is a curious and widespread tendency among engineers to surround the answer to a simple question with so many preliminaries and commentaries that the answer itself can hardly be discerned. It is so difficult to get a direct answer out of some men that their usefulness is thereby greatly diminished. The tendency is to explain the answer before answering the question. To be sure, very few questions admit of simple answers without qualifications, but the important thing is to state the crux of the matter as succinctly as possible first. On the other hand, there are times when it is very important to add the pertinent background or other relevant facts to illuminate a simple statement. The trick is to convey the maximum of significant information in the minimum time, a valuable asset to any man.

An excellent guide in this respect may be found in the standard practice of newspapers in printing the news. The headlines give 90 per cent of the basic facts. If you have the time and the interest to read further, the first paragraph will give you most of the important particulars. Succeeding paragraphs simply give details of progressively diminishing significance. To fit an article into available space, the editor simply lops off paragraphs from the rear end, knowing that relatively little of importance will be lost. You can hardly do better than to adopt this method in your own reports, presenting your facts in the order of importance, as if you might be cut off any minute.

Be extremely careful of the accuracy of your statements. This seems almost trite, and yet many engineers lose the confidence of their superiors and associates by habitually guessing when they do not know the answer to a direct question. It is certainly important to be able to answer questions concerning your responsibilities, but a wrong answer is worse than no answer. If you do not know, say so, but also say, "I'll find out right away." If you are not certain, indicate the exact degree of certainty or approximation upon which your answer is based. A reputation for dependability and reliability can be one of your most valuable assets.

This applies, of course, to written matter, calculations, etc., as well as to oral reports. It is definitely bad business to submit a report to the boss for approval without first carefully checking it yourself, and yet formal reports are sometimes turned in full of glaring errors and omissions.

IN RELATION TO THE BOSS

Every executive must know what's going on in his bailiwick. This principle is so elementary and fundamental as to be axiomatic. It follows from the very obvious fact that a man cannot possibly manage his business successfully unless he knows what's going on in it. It applies to minor executives and other individuals charged with specific responsibilities as well as to department heads. No one in his right mind will deny the soundness of the principle and yet it is very commonly violated or overlooked. It is cited here because several of the rules which follow are concerned with specific violations of this cardinal requirement.

Do not overlook the fact that you're working for your boss. This sounds simple enough, but some engineers never get it. By all means, you're working for society, the company, the depart-

7

ment, your family, and yourself, but primarily you should be working for and through your boss. And your boss is your immediate superior, to whom you report directly. As a rule, you can serve all other ends to best advantage by working for him, assuming that he's approximately the man he ought to be. It is not uncommon for young engineers, in their impatient zeal to get things done, to ignore the boss, or attempt to go over or around him. Sometimes they move a little faster that way, for a while, but sooner or later they find that such tactics cannot be tolerated in a large organization. Generally speaking, you cannot get by the boss; he determines your rating and he rates you on your ability to cooperate, among other things. Besides, most of us get more satisfaction out of our jobs when we're able to give the boss our personal loyalty, with the feeling that we're helping him to get the main job done.

Be as particular as you can in the selection of your boss. In its effect upon your engineering career, this is second in importance only to the selection of proper parents. In most engineering organizations the influence of the senior engineer, or even the section head, is a major factor in molding the professional character of younger engineers. Long before the days of universities and textbooks, master craftsmen in all the arts absorbed their skills by apprenticeship to master craftsmen. It is very much as in the game of golf; a beginner who constantly plays in company with "dubs" is very apt to remain a "dub" himself, no matter how faithfully he studies the rules, whereas even a few rounds with a "pro" will usually improve a novice's game.

But, of course, it is not always possible to choose your boss advisedly. What if he turns out to be somewhat less than half the man he ought to be? There are only two proper alternatives open to you; (*a*) accept him as the representative of a higher authority and execute his policies and directives as effectively as possible, or (*b*) transfer to some other outfit at the first opportunity. A great deal of mischief can be done to the interests of all concerned (including the company) if some other alternative is elected, particularly in the case of younger men. Consider the damage to the efficiency of a military unit when the privates, disliking the leader, ignore or modify orders to suit their individual notions! To be sure, a business organization is not a military machine, but it is not a mob, either.

One of the first things you owe your boss is to keep him informed of all significant developments. This is a corollary of the preceding rules: An executive must know what's going on. The main question is: How much must he know—how many of the details? This is always a difficult matter for the new man to get straight. Many novices hesitate to bother the boss with too many reports, and it is certainly true that it can be overdone in this direction, but in by far the majority of cases the executive's problem is to extract enough information to keep adequately posted. For every time he has to say, "Don't bother me with so many details," there will be three times he will say, "Why doesn't someone tell me these things?" Bear in mind that he is constantly called upon to account for, defend, and explain your activities to the "higher-ups," as well as to co-ordinate these activities into a larger plan. In a nutshell, the rule is therefore to give him promptly all the information he needs for these two purposes.

Whatever the boss wants done takes top priority. You may think you have more important things to do first, but unless you obtain permission it is usually unwise to put any other project ahead of a specific assignment from your own boss. As a rule, he has good reasons for wanting his job done *now*, and it is apt to have a great deal more bearing upon your rating than less conspicuous projects which may appear more urgent.

Also, make a note of this: If you are instructed to do something and you subsequently decide it isn't worth doing (in view of new data or events) do not just let it die, but inform the boss of your intentions and reasons. Neglect of this point has caused trouble on more than one occasion.

Do not be too anxious to follow the boss's lead. This is the other side of the matter covered by the preceding rule. An undue subservience or deference to the department head's wishes is fairly common among young engineers. A man with this kind of psychology may:

1 Plague the boss incessantly for minute directions and approvals.

2 Surrender all initiative and depend upon the boss to do all of his basic thinking for him.

3 Persist in carrying through a design or a program even after new evidence has proved the original plan to be wrong.

This is where an engineering organization differs from an army. In general, the program laid down by the department or section head is tentative, rather than sacred, and is intended to serve only until a better program is proposed and approved.

The rule therefore is to tell your boss what you have done, at reasonable intervals, and ask his approval of any well-considered and properly planned deviations or new projects that you may have conceived.

REGARDING RELATIONS WITH ASSOCIATES AND OUTSIDERS

Never invade the domain of any other division without the knowledge and consent of the executive in charge. This is a very common offense, which causes no end of trouble. Exceptions will occur in respect to minor details, but the rule applies particularly to:

1 The employment of a subordinate. Never offer a man a job, or broach the matter at all, without first securing the permission of his boss. There may be excellent reasons why the man should not be disturbed.

2 Engaging the time or committing the services of a subordinate for some particular project or trip. How would you feel, after promising in a formal meeting to assign one of your men to an urgent project, to discover that some other executive had had the gall to send him on an out-of-town trip without attempting to notify you? Yet it has been done!

3 Dealings with customers or outsiders, with particular reference to making promises or commitments involving another division. In this connection bear in mind especially that, when you are in the "field" or the "districts," you are in the premises of the district manager or local office, and that all transactions must be with the manager's permission just as if you were in his home.

4 Performing any function assigned to another division or individual. Violations of this law often cause bitter resentments and untold mischief. The law itself is based upon three underlying principles:

(*a*) Most people strongly dislike having anyone "muscle" into their territory, undermining their job by appropriating their functions.

(*b*) Such interference breeds confusion and mistakes. The man in charge of the job usually knows much more about it than you do, and, even when you think you know enough about it, the chances are better than even that you'll overlook some important factor.

(*c*) Nine times out of ten when you're performing the other fellow's function you're neglecting your own. It is rarely that any engineer or executive is so caught up on his own responsibilities that he can afford to take on those of his colleagues.

There is a significant commentary on this last principle which should also be observed: In general you will get no credit or thanks for doing the other fellow's job for him at the expense of your own. But it frequently happens that, if you can put your own house in order first, an understanding of and an active interest in the affairs of other divisions will lead to promotion to a position of greater responsibility. Many a man has been moved up primarily because of a demonstrated capacity for taking care of other people's business as well as his own.

In all transactions be careful to "deal-in" everyone who has a right to be in. It is extremely easy, in a large corporation, to overlook the interests of some division or individual who does not happen to be represented, or in mind, when a significant step is taken. Very often the result is that the step has to be retracted or else considerable damage is done. Even when it does no apparent harm, most people do not like to be left out when they have a stake in the matter, and the effect upon morale may be serious.

Of course there will be times when you cannot wait to stand on ceremony and you'll have to go ahead and "damn the torpedoes." But you cannot do it with impunity too often.

Note particularly that in this and the preceding item the chief offense lies in the invasion of the other man's territory without his knowledge and consent. You may find it expedient on occasions to do the other man's job for him, in order to get your own work done, but you should first give him a fair chance to deliver the goods or else agree to have you take over. If you must offend in this respect, at least you should realize that you are being offensive.

Be careful about whom you mark for copies of letters, memos, etc., when the interests of other departments are involved. A lot of mischief has been caused by young men broadcasting memoranda containing damaging or embarrassing statements. Of course it is sometimes difficult for a novice to recognize the "dynamite" in such a document but, in general, it is apt to cause trouble if it steps too heavily upon someone's toes or reveals a serious shortcoming on anybody's part. If it has wide distribution or if it concerns manufacturing or customer difficulties, you'd better get the boss to approve it before it goes out unless you're very sure of your ground.

Promises, schedules, and estimates are necessary and important instruments in a well-ordered business. Many engineers fail to realize this, or habitually try to dodge the irksome responsibility for making commitments. You *must* make promises based upon your own estimates for the part of the job for which you are responsible, together with estimates obtained from contributing departments for their parts. No one should be allowed to avoid the issue by the old formula, "I can't give a promise because it depends upon so many uncertain factors." Consider the "uncertain factors" confronting a department head who must make up a budget for an entire engineering department for a year in advance! Even the most uncertain case can be narrowed down by first asking, "Will it be done in a matter of a few hours or a few months—a few days or a few weeks?" It usually turns out that it cannot be done in less than three weeks and surely will not require more than five, in which case you'd better say four weeks. This allows one week for contingencies and sets you a reasonable bogie under the comfortable figure of five weeks. Both extremes are bad; a good engineer will set schedules which he can meet by energetic effort at a pace commensurate with the significance of the job.

As a corollary of the foregoing, you have a right to insist upon having estimates from responsible representatives of other departments. But in accepting promises, or statements of facts, it is frequently important to make sure that you are dealing with a properly qualified representative of the other section. Also bear in mind that when you ignore or discount another man's promises you impugn his responsibility and incur the extra liability yourself. Of course this is sometimes necessary, but be sure that you do it advisedly. Ideally, another man's promises should be negotiable instruments, like his personal check, in compiling estimates.

When you are dissatisfied with the services of another section, make your complaint to the individual most directly responsible for the function involved. Complaints made to a man's superiors, over his head, engender strong resentments and should be resorted to only when direct appeal fails. In many cases such complaints are made without giving the man a fair chance to correct the grievance, or even before he is aware of any dissatisfaction.

This applies particularly to individuals with whom you are accustomed to deal directly or at close range, or in cases where you know the man to whom the function has been assigned. It is more formal and in some instances possibly more correct to file a complaint with the head of section or department, and it will no doubt tend to secure prompt results. But there are more than a few individuals who would never forgive you for complaining to their boss without giving them a fair chance to take care of the matter.

Next to a direct complaint to the top, it is sometimes almost as serious an offense to mark a man's boss for a copy of a letter containing a complaint or an implied criticism. Of course the occasion may justify such criticism; just be sure you know what you're doing.

In dealing with customers and outsiders remember that you represent the company, ostensibly with full responsibility and authority. You may be only a few months out of college but most outsiders will regard you as a legal, financial, and technical agent of your company in all transactions, so be careful of your commitments.

2

Relating Chiefly to Engineering Executives

The following is a partial list of basic commandments, readily subscribed to by all executives but practiced only by the really good ones:

INDIVIDUAL BEHAVIOR AND TECHNIQUE

Every Executive must know what's going on in his bailiwick. This is repeated here for emphasis, and because it belongs at the head of the list for this section. Just remember that it works both ways, as regards what you owe your associates and subordinates as well as yourself.

Obviously this applies primarily to major or significant developments and does not mean that you should attempt to keep up with all the minor details of functions assigned to subordinates. It becomes a vice when carried to the extent of impeding operations. Nevertheless, the basic fact remains that the more information an executive has, the more effectively he can manage his business.

Do not try to do it all yourself. This is another one of those elementary propositions that everyone will endorse and yet violations are quite common. It's *bad* business; bad for you, bad for the job, and bad for your men. You *must* delegate responsibility even if you *could* cover all of the ground yourself. It isn't wise to have so much depend upon one man and it's very unfair to your men. It is often said that every executive should have his business so organized that he

15

could take a month's vacation at any time and have everything go along smoothly. The most common excuse for hogging the whole job is that subordinates are too young or inexperienced. It's part of your job to develop your men, which includes developing initiative, resourcefulness, and judgment. The best way to do this is to load them up with all the responsibility they can carry without danger of serious embarrassment to the department. Any self-respecting engineer resents being babied, to the extent where he cannot act on the most trivial detail without express approval of the department head.

On the other hand, it must be granted that details are not always trivial and it may sometimes require a meeting of the management committee to change the length of a screw in a critical piece of mechanism in high production. It's simply a matter of making sure that all items are handled by men of appropriate competence and experience.[1]

Put first things first, in applying yourself to your job. Since there usually isn't time for everything, it is essential to form the habit of concentrating on the important things first. The important things are the things for which you are held directly responsible and accountable, and if you aren't sure what these are you'd better find out mighty quick and fix them clearly in mind. Assign these responsibilities top priority in budgeting your time; then delegate as many as possible of the items which will not fit into your schedule. It is a good general rule never to undertake any minor project or chore that you can get someone else or some other department to do for you, so long as it is not an essential part of your job. For example, if your job is building motors it's a mistake to spend time designing special vibration or sound meters

[1] "Administrative Organization for a Small Manufacturing Firm," by Willis Rabbe, MECHANICAL ENGINEERING, vol. 63, 1941, pp. 517–520.

for testing them if you can get the laboratory to do it for you.

In handling special problems of this sort, it is usually good diplomacy to let some local office do the job, if they can, before importing experts from another plant or company.

The practice of drawing upon all available resources for assistance can frequently be applied to advantage in respect to your major products, as well as in minor details. This is especially true in a large organization where the services of experts, consulting engineers, laboratories, and other departments are available either at no cost or for much less than it would cost you to get the answer independently. In fact, there may well be cases in which it would be wise for you to limit yourself, personally or as a business manager, to performing only those functions to which you can bring some special talent, skill, or contribution, or in which you enjoy some natural advantage. Some companies, for example, have achieved outstanding success by virtue of their special genius for merchandising the products of others, or by concentrating on the manufacture of a standard competitive article so as to capture the market by lowering the price. Likewise the aircraft companies generally exploit their special aeronautical skill, leaving development of engines, superchargers, propellers, and other components to specialists in these fields. Few of us are versatile enough to excel in more than one or two talents.

Cultivate the habit of "boiling matters down" to their simplest terms. The faculty for reducing apparently complicated situations to their basic, essential elements is a form of wisdom that must usually be derived from experience, but there are marked differences between otherwise comparable individuals in this respect. Some people seem eternally disposed to "muddy the water;" or they "can never see the woods for the trees," etc. Perhaps a man cannot correct such an innate tendency simply by taking thought, but it appears to be largely a matter of habit, a habit of withdrawing mentally to a suitable vantage point so as to survey a mass of facts in their proper perspective, or a habit of becoming immersed and lost in a sea of detail. Make it practice to integrate, condense, summarize, and simplify your facts rather than to expand, ramify, complicate, and disintegrate them.

Many meetings, for example, get nowhere after protracted wrangling until somebody finally says "Well, gentlemen, it all boils down simply to this, . . .", or "Can't we agree, however, that the basic point at issue is just this, ...", or, "After all, the essential fact remains that . . . ."

This sort of mental discipline, which instinctively impels a man to go down to the core to get at the crux of the matter, is one of the most valuable qualities of a good executive.[2]

Do not get excited in engineering emergencies—keep your feet on the ground. This is certainly trite enough, and yet an engineering group will sometimes be thrown into a state of agitation bordering on panic by some minor crisis. This refers especially to bad news from the factory or the field regarding some serious and embarrassing difficulty, such as an epidemic of equipment failures. Most crises aren't half as bad as they appear at first, so make it a point to minimize rather than magnify a bad situation. Do not ignore signs of trouble and get caught napping, but learn to distinguish between isolated cases and real epidemics. The important thing is to get the facts first, as promptly and as directly as possible. Then act as soon as you have enough evidence from responsible sources to enable you to reach a sound decision.

Engineering meetings should not be too large or too small. Many executives carry their aversion for large meetings to the point of a phobia. This is reflected in the common saying that nothing worth while is ever accomplished in a large meeting. It is true enough that large meetings frequently

---

[2] See also: "Psychology for Executives," by Elliott Dunlap Smith, Harper & Bros., New York, N. Y., 1935.

dissipate the subject over a number of conflicting or irrelevant points of view, in a generally superficial manner. But this is almost entirely a matter of the competence of the chairman. A considerable amount of skill is required to manage a sizable meeting so as to keep it on the proper subject, avoiding long-winded digressions or reiterations of the arguments. It should be the function of the chairman, or the presiding senior executive, to bring out the pertinent facts bearing upon the matter, in their logical order, and then to secure agreement upon the various issues by (*a*) asking for general assent to concrete proposals, or (*b*) taking a vote, or (*c*) making arbitrary decisions. Engineering meetings may degenerate into protracted wrangles for lack of competent direction. The danger in this respect seems to be about in proportion to the size of the meeting.

Small meetings, three or four persons, can usually hammer out a program or dispose of knotty problems much more effectively. The chief drawback lies in the possibility that all interested parties may not be represented, and considerable loss or mischief may result from failure to take account of significant facts or points of view. Apart from the actual loss involved, strong resentment or discouragement may be engendered in the neglected parties. (The Revolutionary War was brought about largely as a result of the fact that the Colonies were not represented in the British Parliament.)

There will doubtless be cases in which it is neither feasible nor desirable to have all interested parties represented in engineering discussions, particularly if the participants are well informed. But in general it is fitting, proper, and helpful to have the man present whose particular territory is under discussion.

An excellent expedient for avoiding the objections to either extreme in this respect is to keep the meeting small, calling in each keyman when his particular responsibility is being discussed.

19

In any kind of a meeting the important thing is to face the issues and dispose of them. All too often there is a tendency to dodge the issues, postponing action until a later date, or "letting the matter work itself out naturally." Matters will always work out "naturally" if the executive function of control is neglected but this represents a low order of "management." Count any meeting a failure which does not end up with a definite understanding as to what's going to be done; who's going to do it, and when. This should be confirmed in writing (minutes).

Cultivate the habit of making brisk, clean-cut decisions. This is, of course, the most difficult and important part of an executive's job. Some executives have a terrific struggle deciding even minor issues, mainly because they never get over being afraid of making mistakes. Normally, facility comes with practice, but it can be hastened by observing a few simple principles.

1 Decisions will be easier and more frequently correct if you have the essential facts at hand. It will therefore pay you to keep well informed, or else to bring out the relevant facts before attempting a decision. However, it is sometimes said that anybody can make decisions when all of the facts are at hand, whereas an executive will make the same decisions without waiting for the facts.[3] To maintain a proper balance in this respect, when in doubt ask yourself the question: "Am I likely to lose more by giving a snap judgment or by waiting for more information?"

2 The application of judgment can be facilitated by formulating it into principles, policies, and precepts in advance. The present paper is an attempt to formulate experience for this purpose. Make up your own code, if you will, but at least have some sort of code, for much the same reason that

---

[3] See "Definition of an Executive," by H. S. Osborne, *Electrical Engineering*, vol. 61, August, 1942, p. 429.

you memorize the axioms of Euclid or Newton's laws of motion.

3   You do not have to be right every time. It is said that a good executive needs to be right only 51 per cent of the time (although a little better margin would obviously be healthy).

4   The very fact that a decision is difficult usually means that the advantages and drawbacks of the various alternatives are pretty well balanced, so that the net loss cannot amount to much in any event. In such cases it is frequently more important to arrive at some decision—any decision—promptly than to arrive at the best decision ultimately. So take a definite position and see it through.

5   It is futile to try to keep everybody happy in deciding issues involving several incompatible points of view. By all means give everyone a fair hearing, but after all parties have had their say and all facts are on the table, dispose of the matter decisively even if someone's toes are stepped on. Otherwise the odds are that all parties will end up dissatisfied, and even the chief beneficiary will think less of you for straddling the issue.

The following criteria are helpful in choosing a course of action when other factors are indecisive; ask yourself these questions:

(*a*)   Does it expedite and progress the undertaking, or does it smack of procrastination and delay?

(*b*)   Is it fair and square and aboveboard?

(*c*)   Is it in line with established custom, precedence, or policy? A good reason is generally required for a departure.

(*d*)   Is it in line with a previous specific decision or understanding? Even a good reason for making a change will sometimes not offset the unfortunate impression of apparent instability. "He can't make up his own mind" is a common reaction. (Observe, however, that this criterion is suggested only "when other factors are indecisive." By all means have the courage of your convictions when the change is justifiable.)

(e) What are the odds? Can I afford to take the chance? How does the possible penalty compare with the possible gain, in each of the alternatives offered? Very often you can find a solution wherein the worst possible eventuality isn't too bad, in relation to the possible gains.

Do not allow the danger of making a mistake to inhibit your initiative to the point of "nothing ventured, nothing gained." It is much healthier to expect to make mistakes, take a few good risks now and then, and take your medicine when you lose. Moreover, there are few mistakes that cannot be turned into profit somehow, even if it's only in terms of experience.

Finally, it should be observed that having "the courage of your convictions" includes having the courage to do what you know to be right, technically as well as morally, without undue regard for possible criticism or the necessity for explaining your actions. Many seemingly embarrassing situations can readily be cleared up, or even turned to advantage, merely by stating the simple, underlying facts of the matter. It boils down to a very straightforward proposition. If your reasons for your actions are sound, you should not worry about having to defend them to anyone; if they're not sound you'd better correct them promptly, instead of building up an elaborate camouflage.

Do not overlook the value of suitable "preparation" before announcing a major decision or policy. When time permits, it is frequently good diplomacy to prepare the ground for such announcements by discussing the matter in advance with various keymen or directly interested parties. This is, in fact, an elementary technique in diplomatic and political procedure, but it is all too often ignored in engineering practice. Much embarrassment and bad feeling can be caused by announcing a major change or embarking upon a new program or policy without consulting those directly affected or who are apt to bring up violent objections, with good reason later on.[4]

HANDLING DESIGN AND DEVELOPMENT PROJECTS

Beware of the "perils of security" in planning your engineering programs. It is one of the fundamental anomalies of human experience that too much preoccupation with the pursuit of security is very apt to lead to greater danger and insecurity. In a competitive world you *must* take chances—bold and courageous chances—or else the other fellow will, and he will win out just enough often to keep you running, all out of breath, trying to catch up. So it behooves you as an engineering executive to "stick your neck out," and keep it out, by undertaking stiff development programs, setting a high mark to shoot at, and then working aggressively to realize your objectives. With competent direction any representative engineering organization will work its way out of a tight spot, every time, under the pressure of the emergency. If you do not like such "emergencies," just remember that, if you do not create your own emergencies in advance, your competition will create them for you at a much more embarrassing time later on.

In order to minimize the risk it is good policy to hedge against the failure of a new project by providing an alternative, or an "out" to fall back on, wherever practicable. You can go after bigger stakes with impunity when you have suitably limited your possible losses in such a manner.

Plan your work, then work your plan. The following formula for carrying out a development or design project seems to be standard in the best engineering circles:

[4] See also: "The Technique of Executive Control," by Erwin Haskell Schell. Fifth edition, Book Co., Inc., New York, N. Y., 1942.

(*a*) Define your objectives.

(*b*) Plan the job, by outlining the steps to be accomplished.

(*c*) Prepare a definite schedule.

(*d*) Assign definite responsibilities for each item.

(*e*) Make sure that each man has sufficient help and facilities.

(*f*) Follow up; check up on progress of the work.

(*g*) Revise your schedule as required.

(*h*) Watch for "bottlenecks," "log-jams," and "missing links;" hit lagging items hard.

(*i*) Drive to a finish on time.

Plan your development work far enough ahead of production so as to meet schedules without a wild last-minute rush. In the nature of things it seems inevitable that the group responsible for design engineering is also in the best position to take care of development projects. This is due to the intimate contacts of the designers with the practical problems of production, performance, and market requirements. But it is also true that very considerable foresight is required to offset the natural tendency of designers to become preoccupied with immediate problems of this nature, at the expense of the long-range development program, which is not so urgent and pressing. It is therefore the function of management to exercise sufficient "vision" to anticipate trends and initiate research and development projects before the demand becomes uncomfortably urgent. This means starting such projects soon enough, i.e., six months, a year, or even two years in advance, to allow sufficient time to carry out all of the necessary steps in a well-ordered program.

Even when the development of new designs simply means a rehash of old fundamentals in new dress, it is important to plan the program early enough and to provide for all stages in the process of getting the product on the market. For ex-

24

ample, the following steps may be required to carry through the development of a typical peacetime product:

(a) Market survey.

(b) Preparation of commercial specifications (features and ratings agreed upon jointly by commercial and design divisions).

(c) Preliminary design.

(d) Build and test preliminary sample.

(e) Final design.

(f) Build and test final samples.

(g) Preliminary planning and costs.

(h) Engineering release of final drawings for production.

(i) Final planning and costs.

(j) Ordering materials and tools.

(k) Preparation of manufacturing and test instructions; application, installation, operating and service manuals; replacement-parts catalogue, publicity releases.

(l) Initial production.

(m) Test production samples.

(n) Minor design changes to correct errors and expedite production.

Obviously, some of these activities can be carried on concurrently, but unless they are all suitably provided for there is very apt to be some awkward stumbling and bungling along the way.

Be careful to "freeze" a new design when the development has progressed far enough. Of course it is not always easy to say how far is "far enough" but, in general, you have gone far enough when you can meet the design specifications and costs, with just enough time left to complete the remainder of the program on schedule. The besetting temptation of the designing engineer is to allow himself to be led on by one glittering improvement after another, pursuing an elusive perfection that leads him far past the hope of ever keeping his promises and commitments. Bear in mind that there will always be new design improvements coming along, but it is usually better to get started with what you have on time, provided only that it is up to specifications as regards features, quality, and cost.

Constantly review developments and other activities to make certain that actual benefits are commensurate with costs in money, time, and manpower. Not infrequently developments are carried along by virtue of Newton's first law of motion long after they have ceased to yield a satisfactory return on the investment. The occasion for vigilance in this respect is obvious enough; it is cited here simply as a reminder.

Make it a rule to require, and submit, regular periodic progress reports, as well as final reports on completed projects. However irksome such chores may seem, your business simply isn't fully organized and controlled until you have established this practice, as regards reports to your superiors as well as from your subordinates. There appears to be no other regimen quite so compelling and effective in requiring a man to keep his facts properly assembled and appraised.

It is further true that, generally speaking, an engineering project is not really finished until it is properly summarized, recorded, and filed in such a manner that the information can readily be located and utilized by all interested parties. An enormous amount of effort can be wasted or duplicated in any engineering department when this sort of information is simply entrusted to the memory of individual engineers.

NOTES RESPECTING ORGANIZATION[5]

Do not have too many men reporting directly to one man. As a rule, not more than six or seven men should report to one exec-

―――

[5] For a more authoritative discussion of this subject, see the excellent series of papers on "Organization and Management of Engineering," *Electrical Engineering*, vol. 61, Aug. 1942, pp. 422–429.

utive in an engineering organization. Occasionally a strong energetic leader will deal directly with fifteen or twenty engineers, in which case he is usurping the positions and functions of several group leaders, burdening himself with too much detail, and depriving the men of adequate supervision.

Assign definite responsibilities. It is extremely detrimental to morale and efficiency when no one knows just what his job is or what he is responsible for. If assignments are not made clear there is apt to be interminable bickering, confusion, and bad feeling. Do not keep tentative organization changes hanging over people. It is better to dispose of a situation promptly, and change it later, than to hold up a decision simply because you might want to change it. It is again a matter of facing issues squarely; it is easier to "just wait and see how things work out" but, beyond the minimum time required to size up personnel, it's not good management.

In so far as possible, avoid divided responsibility for specific functions. Ideally each man should have full authority and control over all of the factors essential to the performance of his particular function. This is commonly expressed in the aphorism that authority must be commensurate with responsibility. In practice this is seldom possible of fulfillment; we must all depend upon the contributions of others at some point in the process. Still the amount of dependency should be kept to the practical minimum, for it is extremely difficult for a man to get anything done if he must eternally solicit the voluntary co-operation or approval of too many other parties. This is what is known as being "organized to prevent things from getting done."

The logical answer to the problem of divided responsibility (or "division of labor") is co-ordination. If any activity, such as the design of a product, must be divided into development, design, drafting, and production engineering, these

functions should obviously be co-ordinated by a single responsible engineer.

If you haven't enough legal authority assume as much as you need.
During the Civil War a Confederate officer one evening found
that his supply train was held up by a single Union battery
which was dropping shells accurately into a narrow moun-
tain pass. Without even changing his uniform, he rode
around to the rear of the battery, and coming upon them
suddenly, sharply ordered them to swing their guns around
to another point. He was obeyed with alacrity because he
acted as if he expected to be obeyed. He rode off to rejoin
his command, and led them through the pass before anyone
discovered that he had exceeded his authority.

Of course such tactics are not recommended for general use,
but the story illustrates the fact that quite a lot can be accomplished, on occasions, without full administrative sanction.
The important thing is to exercise sufficient care to avoid
running afoul of the interests and authority of others.

This injunction is based upon three elementary facts of
experience:

1 A man will frequently be held responsible for a good
deal more than he can control by directly delegated authority.

2 A very considerable amount of authority can be assumed with complete impunity if it is assumed discreetly,
and with effective results. People in general tend to obey a
man who appears to be in charge of any situation, provided
that he appears to know what he is doing and obtains the
desired results.

3 Most executives will be very pleased to confirm such authority in their subordinates when they see it being exer-
cised effectively. Executives in general have much more
trouble pushing their men ahead than in holding them back.

Do not create "bottlenecks." Co-ordination of minor routine affairs is sometimes carried too far, when a single individual must pass upon each transaction before it can be carried out. Such rigid control can easily cause more trouble than the original liability. Fortunately, bottlenecks are usually recognized early in the game, and it is easy to avoid them by designating alternates, or by allowing freedom of action in emergencies, with the proviso that the proper party be notified at the first opportunity.

Assign responsibilities for technical subjects, as well as for specific products, in setting up your engineering organization. This is a practice which could be used to advantage in design sections more frequently than it is. The idea is to assign dual responsibilities to each engineer; (*a*) for a particular product or line of apparatus, and (*b*), for a technical specialty, such as lubrication, heat transfer, surface finishes, magnetic materials, welding, fluid flow, etc. These assignments should be made known to all members of the group, with the request that all pertinent material on each subject be referred to the proper specialist, who will act as consultant and as contact man with laboratories, etc., for the entire section. It may, of course, be desirable to assign full-time specialists to important subjects when the business can afford it; the main point is to establish pools of specialized knowledge rather than to expect each designer to know all that he needs to know about the principal arts and sciences which are common to the various products of the department.

WHAT EVERY EXECUTIVE OWES HIS MEN

Promote the personal and professional interests of your men on all occasions. This is not only an obligation, it is the opportunity and the privilege of every executive.

As a general principle, the interests of individual engineers coincide with the company's interest, i.e., there is, or should be, no basic conflict. The question of which should be placed first is, therefore, rarely encountered in practice, although it is clear that, in general, the company's interests, like those of the state or society, must take precedence. It is one of the functions of management to reconcile and merge the two sets of interests to their mutual advantage, since they are so obviously interdependent.

It should be obvious that it is to the company's advantage to preserve the morale and loyalty of individual engineers, just as it is common policy to maintain proper relations with the labor unions. The fact is that attempts to organize engineers into unions have failed simply because the engineers have been confident that their interests have been looked after very conscientiously and very adequately by responsible executives.

Morale is a tremendously important factor in any organization. It is founded primarily upon confidence, and it reaches a healthy development when the men feel that they will always get a square deal plus a little extra consideration on occasions.

Specific injunctions under this principle are cited in succeeding items.

Do not hang onto a man too selfishly when he is offered a better opportunity elsewhere. It's a raw deal to stand in the way of a man's promotion just because it will inconvenience you to lose him. You are justified in shielding him from outside offers only when you are sincerely convinced that he has an equal or better opportunity where he is. Moreover, you should not let yourself get caught in a position where the loss of any man would embarrass you unduly. Select and train runners-up for all keymen, including yourself.

Do not short-circuit or override your men if you can possibly avoid it. It is very natural, on occasions, for an executive to want to exercise his authority directly in order to dispose of a matter promptly without regard for the man assigned to the job. To be sure, it's your prerogative, but it can be very demoralizing to the subordinate involved and should be resorted to only in real emergencies. Once you give a man a job, let him do it, even at the cost of some inconvenience to yourself. Never miss a chance to build up the prestige of your men. And more than a little mischief can be done by exercising authority without sufficient knowledge of the details of the matter.

You owe it to your men to keep them properly informed. Next to responsibility without authority comes responsibility without information, in the catalogue of raw deals. It is very unfair to expect a man to acquit himself creditably when he is held responsible for a project without adequate knowledge of its past history, present status, or future plans. An excellent practice, followed by many top-flight executives, is to hold occasional meetings of section heads to acquaint them with major policies and developments in the business of the department and the company, so that all will know what's going on.

An important part of the job of developing a man is to furnish him with an ample background of information in his particular field, and as a rule this involves a certain amount of travel. There are occasions when it is worth while to send a young man along on a trip for what he can get out of it, rather than what he can contribute to the job.

Do not criticize one of your men in front of others, especially his own subordinates. This obviously damages prestige and morale.

Also, be very careful not to criticize a man when it's really your own fault. Not infrequently, the real offense can be traced back to you, as when you fail to advise, or warn, or train the man properly. Be fair about it.

Show an interest in what your men are doing. It is definitely discouraging to a man when his boss manifests no interest in his work, as by failing to inquire, comment, or otherwise take notice of it.

Never miss a chance to commend or reward a man for a job well done. Remember that your job is not just to criticize and browbeat your men into getting their work done. A first-rate executive is a leader as well as a critic. The better part of your job is, therefore, to help, advise, encourage, and stimulate your men.

On the other hand, this does not mean mollycoddling. By all means get tough when the occasion justifies it. An occasional sharp censure, when it is well deserved, will usually help to keep a man on his toes. But if that's all he gets, he is apt to go a bit sour on the job.

Always accept full responsibility for your group and the individuals in it. Never "pass the buck," or blame one of your men, even when he has "let you down" badly, in dealings with outsiders. You are supposed to have full control and you are credited with the success as well as the failure of your group.

Do all that you can to see that each of your men gets all of the salary that he's entitled to. This is the most appropriate reward or compensation for outstanding work, greater responsibility, or increased value to the company. (Any recommendation for an increase in salary must be justified on one of these three bases.)

Include interested individuals in introductions, luncheons, etc., when entertaining visitors. Obviously, this can be overdone, but if you're entertaining a visiting specialist, it is good business, as well as good manners, to invite the corresponding specialist in your own department to go along.

Do all that you can to protect the personal interests of your men and their families, especially when they're in trouble. Do not confine your interest in your men rigidly within the boundaries of "company business."

32

Try to get in little extra accommodations when justifiable. For example, if you're sending a man to his home town on a business trip, schedule it for Monday, so that he can spend Sunday with his family, if it makes no difference otherwise.

Considerations of this sort make a "whale" of a difference in the matter of morale and in the satisfaction an executive gets out of his job. The old-fashioned "slave driver" is currently regarded in about the same light as Heinrich Himmler. Treat your men as human beings making up a team rather than as cogs in a machine.

In this connection, it is sometimes advisable to talk things over with a man when you become definitely dissatisfied with his work, or recognize a deficiency which is militating against him. To be sure, it is not always easy, and may require much tact to avoid discouraging or offending the man, but it may well be that you owe it to him. Bear this in mind; if you ultimately have to fire him, you may have to answer two pointed questions: "Why has it taken you five years to discover my incompetence?" and, "Why haven't you given me a fair chance to correct these shortcomings?" Remember that when you fire a man for incompetence, it means not only that he has failed, but also that you have failed.

3

Purely Personal Considerations for Engineers

The importance of the personal and sociological aspects of our behavior as engineers is brought out in the following quotation (1):[6]

"In a recent analysis of over 4000 cases, it was found that 62 per cent of the employees discharged were unsatisfactory because of social unadaptability, only 38 per cent for technical incompetence."

And yet about 99 per cent of the emphasis in the training of engineers is placed upon purely technical or formal education. In recent years, however, there has been a rapidly growing appreciation of the importance of "human engineering," not only in respect to relations between management and employees but also as regards the personal effectiveness of the individual worker, technical or otherwise. It should be obvious enough that a highly trained technological expert with a good character and personality is necessarily a better engineer and a great deal more valuable to his company than a sociological freak or misfit with the same technical training. This is largely a consequence of the elementary fact that in a normal organization no individual can get very far in accomplishing any worth-while objectives without the voluntary co-operation of his associates; and the quantity and quality of such co-operation is determined by the "personality factor" more than anything else.

---

[6] Numbers in parentheses refer to the Bibliography at the end of the paper.

34

This subject of personality and character is, of course, very broad and much has been written and preached about it from the social, ethical, and religious points of view. The following "laws" are drawn up from the purely practical point of view based upon well-established principles of "good engineering practice," or upon consistently repeated experience. As in the preceding sections, the selections are limited to rules which are frequently violated, with unfortunate results, however obvious or bromidic they may appear.

"LAWS" OF CHARACTER AND PERSONALITY

One of the most important personal traits is the ability to get along with all kinds of people. This is rather a comprehensive quality but it defines the prime requisite of personality in any type of industrial organization. No doubt this ability can be achieved by various formulas, although it is probably based mostly upon general, good-natured friendliness, together with fairly consistent observance of the "Golden Rule." The following "do's and don'ts" are more specific elements of such a formula:

1 Cultivate the tendency to appreciate the good qualities, rather than the shortcomings of each individual.

2 Do not give vent to impatience and annoyance on slight provocation. Some offensive individuals seem to develop a striking capacity for becoming annoyed, which they indulge with little or no restraint.

3 Do not harbor grudges after disagreements involving honest differences of opinion. Keep your arguments on an objective basis and leave personalities out as much as possible.

4 Form the habit of considering the feelings and interests of others.

5 Do not become unduly preoccupied with your own selfish interests. It may be natural enough to "look out for Number One first," but when you do your associates will

leave the matter entirely in your hands, whereas they will be much readier to defend your interests for you if you characteristically neglect them for unselfish reasons.

This applies particularly to the matter of credit for accomplishments. It is much wiser to give your principal attention to the matter of getting the job done, or to building up your men, than to spend too much time pushing your personal interests ahead of everything else. You need have no fear of being overlooked; about the only way to lose credit for a creditable job is to grab for it too avidly.

6 Make it a rule to help the other fellow whenever an opportunity arises. Even if you're mean-spirited enough to derive no personal satisfaction from accommodating others it's a good investment. The business world demands and expects co-operation and teamwork among the members of an organization. It's smarter and pleasanter to give it freely and ungrudgingly, up to the point of unduly neglecting your own responsibilities.

7 Be particularly careful to be fair on all occasions. This means a good deal more than just being fair, upon demand. All of us are frequently unfair, unintentionally, simply because we do not habitually view the matter from the other fellow's point of view, to be sure that his interests are fairly protected. For example, when a man fails to carry out an assignment, he is sometimes unjustly criticized when the real fault lies with the executive who failed to give him the tools to do the job. Whenever you enjoy some natural advantage, or whenever you are in a position to injure someone seriously, it is especially incumbent upon you to "lean over backwards" to be fair and square.

8 Do not take yourself or your work too seriously. A normal healthy sense of humor, under reasonable control, is much more becoming, even to an executive, than a chronically soured dead-pan, a perpetually unrelieved air of deadly seriousness, or the pompous solemn dignity of a stuffed owl.

The Chief Executive of the United States smiles easily or laughs heartily, on appropriate occasions, and even his worst enemies do not attempt to criticize him for it. It is much better for your blood pressure, and for the morale of the office, to laugh off an awkward situation now and then than to maintain a tense tragic atmosphere of stark disaster whenever matters take an embarrassing turn. To be sure, a serious matter should be taken seriously, and a man should maintain a quiet dignity as a rule, but it does more harm than good to preserve an oppressively heavy and funereal atmosphere around you.

9   Put yourself out just a little to be genuinely cordial in greeting people. True cordiality is, of course, spontaneous and should never be affected, but neither should it be inhibited. We all know people who invariably pass us in the hall or encounter us elsewhere without a shadow of recognition. Whether this be due to inhibition or preoccupation we cannot help feeling that such unsociable chumps would not be missed much if we never saw them again. On the other hand, it is difficult to think of anyone who is too cordial, although it can doubtless be overdone like anything else. It appears that most people tend naturally to be sufficiently reserved or else overreserved in this respect.

10   Give the other fellow the benefit of the doubt if you are inclined to suspect his motives, especially when you can afford to do so. Mutual distrust and suspicion breed a great deal of absolutely unnecessary friction and trouble, frequently of a very serious nature. This is a very common phenomenon, which can be observed among all classes and types of people, in international as well as local affairs. It is derived chiefly from misunderstandings, pure ignorance, or from an ungenerous tendency to assume that a man is guilty until he is proved innocent. No doubt the latter assumption is the "safer" bet, but it is also true that if you treat the other fellow as a depraved scoundrel, he will usually treat you likewise, and he will

probably try to live down to what is expected of him. On the other hand you will get much better co-operation from your associates and others if you assume that they are just as intelligent, reasonable, and decent as you are, even when you know they're not (although the odds are 50:50 that they are). It isn't a question of being naive or a perpetual sucker; you'll gain more than you lose by this practice, with anything more than half-witted attention to the actual odds in each case.

Do not be too affable. It's a mistake, of course, to try too hard to get along with everybody merely by being agreeable and friendly on all occasions. Somebody will take advantage of you sooner or later, and you cannot avoid trouble simply by running away from it ("appeasement"). You must earn the respect of your associates by demonstrating your readiness to give any man a hell of a good fight if he asks for it. Shakespeare put it succinctly in Polonius' advice to his son (in "Hamlet"): "Beware of entrance to a quarrel; but being in, bear it that the opposed may beware of thee."

On the other hand, do not give ground too quickly just to avoid a fight, when you know you're in the right. If you can be pushed around easily the chances are that you will be pushed around. There will be times when you would do well to start a fight yourself, when your objectives are worth fighting for.

As a matter of fact, as long as you're in a competitive business you're in a fight all the time. Sometimes it's a fight between departments of the same company. As long as it's a good clean fight, with no hitting below the belt, it's perfectly healthy. But keep it on the plane of "friendly competition" as long as you can. (In the case of arguments with your colleagues, it is usually better policy to settle your differences out of court, rather than to take them to the boss for arbitration.)

Likewise, in your relations with subordinates it is unwise to carry friendliness to the extent of impairing discipline. There are times when the best thing that you can do for a man (and the company) is to fire him, or transfer him. Every one of your men should know that whenever he deserves a good "bawling out" he'll get it, every time. The most rigid discipline is not resented so long as it is reasonable, impartial, and fair, especially when it is balanced by appropriate rewards, appreciation, and other compensations as mentioned in Part 2. Too much laxity or squeamishness in handling men is about as futile as cutting off a dog's tail an inch at a time to keep it from hurting so much. If you do not face your issues squarely, someone else will be put in your place who will.

Regard your personal integrity at one of your most important assets. In the long pull there is hardly anything more important to you than your own self-respect and this alone should provide ample incentive to maintain the highest standard of ethics of which you are capable. But, apart from all considerations of ethics and morals, there are perfectly sound hardheaded business reasons for conscientiously guarding the integrity of your character.

One of the most striking phenomena of an engineering office is the transparency of character among the members of any group who have been associated for any length of time. In a surprisingly short period each individual is recognized, appraised, and catalogued for exactly what he is, with far greater accuracy than that individual usually realizes. This is true to such a degree that it makes a man appear downright ludicrous when he assumes a pose or otherwise tries to convince us that he is something better than he is. As Emerson puts it: "What you are speaks so loud I cannot hear what you say." In fact it frequently happens that a man is much better known and understood by his associates, collectively, than he knows and understands himself.

Therefore, it behooves you as an engineer to let your personal conduct, overtly and covertly, represent your conception of the very best practical standard of professional ethics, by which you are willing to let the world judge and rate you.

Moreover, it is morally healthy and tends to create a better atmosphere, if you will credit the other fellow with similar ethical standards, even though you may be imposed upon occasionally. The obsessing and overpowering fear of being cheated is the common characteristic of second- and third-rate personalities. This sort of psychology sometimes leads a man to assume an extremely "cagey" sophisticated attitude, crediting himself with being impressively clever when he is simply taking advantage of his more considerate and fair-minded associates. On the other hand a substantial majority of top-flight executives are scrupulously fair, square, and straightforward in their dealings with all parties. In fact most of them are where they are largely because of this characteristic, which is one of the prime requisites of first-rate leadership.

The priceless and inevitable reward for uncompromising integrity is confidence, the confidence of associates, subordinates, and "outsiders." All transactions are enormously simplified and facilitated when a man's word is as good as his bond and his motives are above suspicion. Confidence is such an invaluable business asset that even a moderate amount of it will easily outweigh any temporary advantage that might be gained by sharp practices.

Integrity of character is closely associated with sincerity, which is another extremely important quality. Obvious and marked sincerity is frequently a source of exceptional strength and influence in certain individuals, particularly in the case of speakers. Abraham Lincoln is a classic example. In any individual, sincerity is always appreciated, and insincerity is quickly detected and discounted.

In order to avoid any misunderstanding, it should be

granted here that the average man, and certainly the average engineer, is by no means a low dishonest scoundrel. In fact the average man would violently protest any questioning of his essential honesty and decency, perhaps fairly enough. But there is no premium upon this kind of common garden variety of honesty, which is always ready to compromise in a pinch. The average man will go off the gold standard or compromise with any sort of expediency whenever it becomes moderately uncomfortable to live up to his obligations. This is hardly what is meant by "integrity," and it is certainly difficult to base even a moderate degree of confidence upon the guarantee that you will not be cheated unless the going gets tough.

A little profanity goes a long way. Engineering is essentially a gentleman's profession, and it ill becomes a man to carry profanity to the point of becoming obnoxiously profane. Unfortunately, profanity is sometimes taken as a mark of rugged he-man virility, but any engineer with such an idea should realize that many a pimply, half-witted, adolescent street urchin will hopelessly outclass him in this respect.

On the other hand, there is no reason why a man should be afraid to say "damn." On appropriate occasions a good hearty burst of colorful profanity may be just a healthy expression of strong feelings. But there is never any occasion for the filthy variety of obscenity, and a really foul mouth will generally inspire nothing but contempt.

Be careful of your personal appearance. Roughly eight out of every ten engineers pay adequate attention to their personal appearance and neatness. The other two offend in respect to one or more of the following items:

1 Suit rumpled or soiled, or else trousers, coat, and vest have nothing in common but their means of support.
2 Shoes, unpolished or dilapidated.
3 Tie, at half-mast or looking like it was tied with one

hand. Some individuals seem to own but one tie, which takes an awful beating. Others wear colors contrasting violently with suit or shirt, but this is sometimes a matter of artistic license (if it isn't color blindness).

4   Shirt, frayed at collar or cuffs, or just plain dirty.

5   Hands, dirty.

6   Nails, in deep mourning, chewed off, or else absurdly long. A man doesn't need to be fastidious, but dirty neglected nails immediately and conspicuously identify a careless sloppy individual. (This is especially true in the case of an interview, where first impressions are so important.)

Of course we all know some very good men who are oblivious to such details, so that it cannot be said that all who ignore them are necessarily crude, third-rate, slovenly lowbrows, but it is probably a safe bet that all crude, third-rate, slovenly low-brows are offensive in most of these respects.

Do not argue that you cannot afford to look your best; you cannot afford not to. Your associates and superiors notice these details, perhaps more than you realize, and they rate you accordingly.

In this connection, note the following quotation from a recent pamphlet on "employee rating" (2):

"The 'halo effect' simply means that rating of one trait is often influenced by that given to some other trait. Thus an employee who makes a nice appearance and has a pleasant manner is apt to obtain a higher rating on all other traits than he deserves."

Analyze yourself and your men. In the foregoing, it has been assumed that any normal individual will be interested in either:

(*a*) Advancement to a position of greater responsibility, or (*b*) improvement in personal effectiveness as regards quantity and/or quality of accomplishment.

Either of these should result in increased financial compensation and satisfaction derived from the job.

With reference to item (*a*), it is all too often taken for granted that increased executive and administrative responsibility is a desirable and appropriate form of reward for outstanding proficiency in any type of work. This may be a mistake from either of two points of view:

1 The individual may be very much surprised to find that he is much less happy in his new job than he thought he was going to be. In many instances young engineers are prone to assume that increased responsibility means mostly increased authority and compensation. Actually, the term "compensation" is well applied, for the extra salary is paid primarily to compensate for the extra burden of responsibility. Of course most people relish the added load, because of the larger opportunities that go with it, but many perfectly normal individuals find it more of a load than anything else. It is not uncommon for an engineer or a scientist to discover, to his dismay, that as soon as he becomes an executive he no longer has time to be an engineer or a scientist. In fact, some executives have time for absolutely nothing else.

2 From the business standpoint, it by no means follows that because a man is a good scientist, he will make a good executive. Many a top-notch technician has been promoted to an administrative position very much to his own and the job's detriment.

These facts should therefore be considered carefully by the man threatened with promotion and by the man about to do the promoting. There are other ways of rewarding a man for outstanding accomplishment.

It is not always easy, however, to decide in advance whether you, or the man in question, would be happier and more effective as an executive or as an individual worker. There is no infallible criterion for this purpose but it will be found that, in general, the two types are distinguished by the characteristics and qualities listed in Table 1.

TABLE 1 CHARACTERISTIC QUALITIES FOR EXECUTIVE OR INDIVIDUAL WORKERS

Executive	Individual worker
Extrovert	Introvert
Cordial, affable	Reserved
Gregarious, sociable	Prefers own company
Likes people	Likes technical work
Interested in people	Interested in mechanisms, ideas
Interested in:	Interested in:
Business	Sciences
Costs	Mathematics
Profit and loss	Literature
Practices	Principles
Ability to get many things done	Ability to get intricate things done
Practical	Idealistic
Extensive (broad perspectives)	Intensive (penetrating)
Synthetist	Analyst
Fast, intuitive	Slow, methodical
Talent for leadership	Independent, self-sufficient
Uses inductive logic	Uses deductive logic
Has competitive spirit	Prefers to "live and let live"
Bold	Modest
Courageous	Retiring
Noisy	Quiet
Aggressive	Restrained
Tough, rugged	Vulnerable, sensitive
Confident	Deferential
Impulsive	Intellectual
Vigorous, energetic	Mediative, philosophical
Opinionated, intolerant	Broad-minded, tolerant
Determined	Adaptable
Impatient	Patient
Enterprising	Conservative

Of course many people represent intermediate types, or mixtures; the attributes given in Table 1 delineate the pronounced types. Nevertheless, if most of your attributes lie in the right-hand column the chances are very much against your becoming a successful executive. On the other hand, if you are interested primarily in increasing your effectiveness as an individual worker you would do well to develop some of the strong qualities listed in the left column, to reinforce the virtues on the right.

Two facts stand out sharply in this connection:

1 Whatever your position, and however complacent you may be about it, there is always room for improving your effectiveness; usually plenty of room.

2 Whatever your natural handicaps may be, it is alway possible to accomplish such improvement by study and practice, provided only that you have the will, the determination, and the interest to sustain the effort.

It is very much like the design of a piece of apparatus. Any experienced engineer knows that it is always possible to secure substantial improvements by a redesign. When you get into it you will find that there are few subjects more absorbing or more profitable than the design and development of a good engineer! As Alexander Pope wrote many years ago:

"The proper study of mankind is man."

As previously suggested, this applies to the development of your men as well as yourself. It likewise applies to the appraisal and selection of men. After your own character, the next most important factor in your ultimate success is the caliber of your assistants. In fact, there are, doubtless, cases where the character of the executive is not particularly important, provided only that he is smart enough to surround himself with top-notch men to carry the load. In many instances the success or failure of your business will depend upon whether your engineers are slightly above or below the marginal level of competence for the industry.

It is a significant fact that, in the overwhelming majority of cases, the decisive differences in the abilities of engineers are relatively small. In spite of the occasional incidence of a genius or a nit-wit, the great majority of personnel in any industry and the backbone of the large organizations are individuals who vary only slightly from the norm. In general, when executives look over an organization to select a man for a better job, those who are passed up have very few actual shortcomings, but the man who is chosen has the least. Likewise, many top executives are distinguished not so much by marked genius as by relative freedom from defects of character. There is nowhere near enough genius to go around.

This should be particularly heartening to the younger men who view the leaders of industry with awe and wonder upon what meat they feed. Nine out of ten of you have "what it takes" as regards native endowments. The problem is to make the most of what you have.

To this end it will be helpful to study some of the employee rating sheets and charts that have been evolved by various industries. Sample forms and a general discussion of the subject will be found in the pamphlet on "employee rating" (2). It is very noticeable that most of these forms are concerned chiefly with acquired rather than inherited traits. The point is that most of the features upon which individuals are rated represent bad habits or plain ignorance, i.e., features that may be controlled and corrected by conscious effort.

CONCLUSION

The foregoing "laws" represent only one basic element in the general formula for a successful engineering career. The complete list of essential components is as follows:

(*a*) The written laws (the arts and sciences).

(*b*) The unwritten laws, of which the foregoing is admittedly no more than a preliminary and very inadequate summary.

(*c*) Native endowments (intelligence, imagination, health, energy, etc.).

(*d*) Luck, chance, opportunities ("the breaks").

The last item is included because good or bad fortune undoubtedly enters into the picture occasionally. Broadly speaking, however, luck tends to average out at a common level over a period of years, and there are more opportunities looking for men than there are men looking for opportunities.

About all that we can do about our native endowments is to conserve, develop, and utilize them to best advantage. The "unwritten laws," including those that are still unwritten, are needed to give direction to our efforts in this latter respect.

The "written laws" receive plenty of attention during our formal schooling, but our studies are not always extended as effectively as they might be after graduation. In many cases, superior technical knowledge and training represent the marginal consideration in the selection of men for key positions.

To anyone interested in improving his professional effectiveness, further study of both types of laws will yield an excellent return on the investment. Under present conditions, however, most engineering graduates are much closer to the saturation point in respect to the written than to the unwritten variety. A few references are listed in the Bibliography for the benefit of those who may be interested in further excursions into these subjects.

Finally it should be observed that the various principles which have been expounded, like those of the arts and sciences, must be assiduously applied and developed in practice if they are to become really effective assets. It is much easier to recognize the validity of these "laws" than it is to apply them consistently, just as it is easier to accept the doctrines of Christianity than to practice them. The important thing here is to select, in so far as possible, a favorable atmosphere for the development of these professional skills. This is undoubtedly one of the major advantages of employment in a large engineering organization, just as it is advantageous to a young doctor to spend his internship in the Mayo Clinic. Perhaps even more important, as previously mentioned, is the selection of your boss, particularly during those first few years that constitute your engineering apprenticeship. No amount of precept is as effective as the proper kind of example. Unfortunately, there is not nearly enough of this kind of example to go around, and in any event it will behoove you to study the "rules of the game" to develop your own set of principles to guide you in your professional practice.

BIBLIOGRAPHY

1 "Elements of Human Engineering," by C. R. Gow, Macmillan Company, New York, N. Y., 1932.

2 "Employee Rating," National Industrial Conference Board, Report 39, New York, N. Y., 1942.

3 "Papers on the Science of Administration," by Luther Gulick and L. Urwick, Institute of Public Administration, Columbia University, New York, N. Y., 1937 (New York State Library, Albany, reference 350.1, qG97).

4 "Principles of Industrial Organization," by D. S. Kimball, McGraw-Hill Book Company, Inc., New York, N. Y., 1933.

5 "Organization and Management in Industry and Business," by W. B. Cornell, The Ronald Press Company, New York, N. Y., 1936.

6 "Industrial Management," by R. H. Lansburgh and W. R. Spriegel, third edition, John Wiley & Sons, Inc., New York, N. Y., 1940.

7 "The Functions of the Executive," by Chester I. Barnard, Harvard University Press, Cambridge, Mass., 1938.

8 "Human Relations Manual for Executives," by Carl Heyel, McGraw-Hill Book Company, Inc., New York, N. Y., 1939.

9 "Organization and Management of Engineering Described at Unusual General Session," reviewing by M. R. Sullivan, R. C. Muir, and H. B. Gear, *Electrical Engineering*, vol. 61, August, 1942, pp. 422–429.

10 "Administrative Organization for a Small Manufacturing Firm," by Willis Rabbe, MECHANICAL ENGINEERING, vol. 63, 1941, pp. 517-520.

11 "Task of the Executive in Modern Industry," by John Airey, *Journal of Engineering Education*, vol. 32, Jan., 1942, pp. 472-479.

12 "Middle Management," by Mary Cushing Howard Niles, Harper & Bro., New York, N. Y., 1941.

13 "Management's Handbook," by L. P. Alford, The Ronald Press Company, New York, N. Y., 1924.

14 "Shop Management," by F. W. Taylor, Harper & Bro., New York, N. Y., 1911. (This is a classic work in which Taylor is credited with laying the foundations of modern "scientific management.")

15 "Onward Industry," by J. D. Mooney and A. C. Riley, Harper & Bro., New York, N. Y., 1931.

16 "Personnel Management and Industrial Relations," by Dale Yoder, Prentice-Hall, Inc., New York, N. Y., 1942.

17 "Industrial Psychology," by Joseph Tiffin, Prentice-Hall, Inc., New York, N. Y., 1942.

18 "Industrial Psychology, Industrial Relations," by Irving Knickerbocker, MECHANICAL ENGINEERING, vol. 65, 1943, pp. 137-138.

19 "What Men Live By," by R. C. Cabot, Houghton-Mifflin Company, New York, N. Y., 1914.

20 "Psychology for Business and Industry," by Herbert Moore, McGraw-Hill Book Company, Inc., New York, N. Y., 1939.

21 "Industrial Management," by G. G. Anderson, M. J. Mandeville, and J. M. Anderson, The Ronald Press Company, New York, N. Y., 1943.

22 "Psychology for Executives," by E. D. Smith, Harper & Bro., New York, N. Y., 1935.

23 "Industrial Relations Handbook," by J. C. Aspley and E. Whitmore, The Dartnell Corporation, Chicago, Ill., 1943.

24 "The Technique of Executive Control," by Erwin Haskell Schell, fifth edition, McGraw-Hill Book Company, Inc., New York, N. Y., 1942.

25 "Management of Manpower," by A. S. Knowles and R. D. Thomson, Macmillan Company, New York, N. Y., 1943.

Recommended Readings

•Technical Analysis of Stock Trends, Robert D. Edwards, John Magee, www.bnpublishing.net

•Wall Street: The Other Las Vegas, Nicolas Darvas, www.bnpublishing.net

•The Anatomy of Success, Nicolas Darvas, www.bnpublishing.net

• The Dale Carnegie Course on Effective Speaking, Personality Development, and the Art of How to Win Friends & Influence People, Dale Carnegie, www.bnpublishing.net

• The Law of Success In Sixteen Lessons by Napoleon Hill (Complete, Unabridged), Napoleon Hill, www.bnpublishing.net

• It Works, R. H. Jarrett, www.bnpublishing.net

•Darvas System for Over the Counter Profits, Nicolas Darvas, www.bnpublishing.net

• The Art of Public Speaking (Audio CD), Dale Carnegie, wwww.bnpublishing.net

• The Success System That Never Fails (Audio CD), W. Clement Stone, www.bnpublishing.net

Printed in the United States
207763BV00001B/340-348/P